Finding Gold in Washington State:

Third Edition -2015

Finding Gold in Washington State:

Third Edition -2015

'SLUICEBOX SEAN' T. TAESCHNER, M.ED.

authorHOUSE®

AuthorHouse™
1663 Liberty Drive
Bloomington, IN 47403
www.authorhouse.com
Phone: 1 (800) 839-8640

Published by AuthorHouse 04/09/2015

ISBN: 978-1-5049-0529-9 (sc)
ISBN: 978-1-5049-0528-2 (e)

Contents

Preface

This book has been an informational guide for hobbyists and serious recreational small scale gold miners in Washington State since 1994.

The guide has answered the questions of WHO/WHAT/WHERE/WHEN/WHY & HOW to find, recover, refine and profit from gold while recreational prospecting.

In addition to answering basic questions for readers, the book has functioned as a field guide explaining common sense mining safety and how to obtain the latest information from Washington State regarding protecting fish and forest resources while prospecting for recoverable gold and other minerals.

The author has also included the hottest areas he has successfully prospected.

Sean's goal has been to enrich every person with the ability to be self-supporting through recreational gold prospecting.

Introduction

More gold was located and recovered in the United States of America between 1930 and 1940 than at any other time in American history, including the gold rushes of 1849 at Sutter's Mill in California and the Klondike Gold Rush of the 1890s in the Alaskan Yukon Territories. What caused this massive rush for gold prior to World War Two? The cause was the Great Depression.

With the hurtful recession of the 21st. Century there has been no doubt that this record may once again have been broken as Americans have lost corporate jobs and sought to self-empower themselves utilizing recreational gold prospecting.

GOLD!

$8.00
Get It Now!

Finding Gold
in
Washington State
by 'Sluicebox Sean' Taeschner ©

WHO/WHAT/WHERE
WHEN/WHY & HOW
TO FIND/RECOVER &
PROFIT FROM GOLD
WHILE RECREATIONAL

IBM DISKETTE
VERSION #2

PROSPECTING!

IN
WASHINGTON
STATE

Corel Draw 4 Illustration

Monica Finds Some Golden Granola at Green River in 2001

Section 1
Gold Separation

Gold has been found in streams and rivers and has deposited itself in cracks and fissures in bedrock, false bedrocks (clays and shales), whirlpool edges, on the downstream-side of rocks and in moss and grasses on the water's edge.

There has been one absolute given in hunting for gold dust or nuggets: where there has been black sand, one will have located gold, platinum, silver, garnet, industrial-grade diamond, arrowheads, fossils, bullets, coins and scrap iron. If any of these items had shown up in a gold pan then one had hit a richly concentrated area. There had been no other area except against a slab's base of bedrock sticking right up out of the water where one located such rich concentrates in black sand!

This led to all of the black sand being saved after it was recovered, most often saved up over a year in five gallon buckets and sold to steel mills for approximately $1500.00/ton. Black sand was made up of hematite, as well as other minerals of gold and silver and platinum too small to see with the naked eye. The goal became demonstrating how to separate the minute minerals from the black sand so that they, too, were not overlooked. With gold at nearly $1,200.00 per troy ounce and platinum at $1,100.00 per troy ounce, it literally paid the small scale miner to reap as much mineral wealth from black sand as possible.

The first step to gold recovery involved removing the larger nuggets of gold from black sand by using eyebrow tweezers. This allowed one to see small pinhead-sized flakes or grains of gold. The best way to separate the gold flakes from the sand was by adding dishwashing soap to the water in the gold pan, having allowed the fish oils and tars holding onto the fine grains of gold the ability to become grease-free; thus, they could not float on top of the water and stick to the black sand. Using warm or hot water worked the best.

PROSPECTORS OFTEN CHANGED THE WATER TWO TO THREE TIMES FOR BEST RESULTS.

The second step involved placing a magnet inside of a plastic-style Ziploc sandwich bag which was then dipped gently into the gold pan. The iron filings in the black sand adhered to the plastic sandwich bag. The bag and its contents were then placed into a nearby bucket of water. Once the magnet was removed from inside of the plastic bag the sand easily dropped off of the sides of the bag and into the bucket.

The third step involved panning off the lighter-weight hematite left behind. The gold flakes were then pushed into a small pile on the pan's bottom after having poured all of the water out. One would then use his thumb, having pressed on the gold, touched to water in a small water-filled vial.

Little glass insulin bottles worked best for saving and viewing concentrates.

The gold sank out rapidly since it was much heavier than lead. Later, the prospector separated the fine black sand left behind along with the gold by allowing the air to dry it out. Having used a small blue, red, or green cereal bowl allowed the prospector to blow gently as fine dust was blown away. Only 24-carat fine grains of gold were left behind. These were placed into a sample vial for storage until sold or melted down by a jeweler or the U.S. Mint. The U.S. Mint only purchased gold that was more than one Troy ounce in weight. Prospectors lost gold that was not insured for a journey to the mint. The U.S. Postal Service became the method of safe shipping.

John Davis at the Green River, 2004.
How Do I Get the Gold Out Now?

Section 2
Black Sand Separation

Magnetite saved in a glass jar or five-gallon buckets by old timers was often crushed with a mortar and pestle into a fine powder and placed into an old iron frying pan (skillet). Adding table salt to the sand (about a half cupful) along with water and a good stir helped separate the gold from the black sand. Only one thing was missing... heat!

This had been where modern day prospectors were known to resurrect methods used by the old time prospectors by using backyard barbecues; these had come in handy as a poor-man's gold refining oven.

Having built a fire in such barbecues with coals that were red to white hot and then having placed the skillet on top became the best known method the old timers effectively used for gold separation.

Waiting until the water had boiled out and the sand and salt were red-hot and producing smoke allowed the old timers a safe method to avoid breathing any toxic fumes coming out of the concentrates.

THIS METHOD WAS VERY DANGEROUS DUE TO THE CYANIDE AND/OR MERCURY FUMES GIVEN OFF DURING THE SEPARATION PROCESS; WHICH, IF BREATHED, COULD KILL A PERSON

INSTANTLY! THEREFORE, THIS PART OF THE SEPARATION WAS DONE OUTDOORS IN A WELL-VENTILATED AREA!

Once the pan of concentrates had turned cherry-red, the old timers used a long one-inch steel pipe about four feet long as an extension handle (so they would not burn themselves) in order to place the pan in a tub of cool water, which made the pan cool rapidly.

The gold would then separate out from the sand and could be panned to remove the fine gold or platinum. Modern day prospectors and miners saved the sand in order to sell it at a local steel mill for $1400.00/ton, about 2,000 pounds equivalent to about (twenty) five-gallon bucket loads of modern iron concentrates.

John Davis Pans Out His Muddy Concentrates, 2004

FACTOID: Today's large nugget gold has sold for $2,500.00/troy ounce, since it has been used in pendant and watchband jewelry making.

Section 3
Gold and Silver Recycling

Old gold jewelry was usually recyclable because it was made up of gold mixed with silver for extra strength. The higher the carat number of gold the softer it would be and the less silver it would contain! Nowadays, most gold jewelry has been a mixture of copper and gold alloy.

Modern day prospectors have been known to use a small hammer and steel block to flatten their gold into a ribbon or large flake to be deposited in a glass jar filled with nitric acid. Having left the gold in the acid for a couple of days allowed the acid to react with the silver in the gold. This method left pure gold precipitating out and the fluid left behind in the jar as silver nitrate (AGNo3).

Allowing the gold to be washed in warm water and left to stand in order to dry for several days in the jar produced a fine gold powder that was sold for $400.00/ounce to jewelers.

The silver nitrate was then recycled as well by dropping several copper pennies into the solution…having been left to sit for a couple of days. This method allowed modern prospectors a concentration of copper nitrate (Cu No3) and pure silver. These prospectors poured off the copper nitrate and allowed the powdered silver to dry for later usage or would leave it in storage for sale at $30.00/troy ounce to chemical supply labs.

Section 4
Melting Down Gold

The Great Depression of the 1930s in the United States of America saw another great gold rush since so many people were out of work and desperate to feed their families. More gold was recovered from 1930 to 1940 than during all previous gold rushes in U.S. history! Until 1930 U.S. dollars had been backed by gold and silver before the U.S. government printed more than we had in storage in national vaults. Since 1930 U.S. money has only been backed by the faith people here and abroad have had in it.

Had it not been for the weekend prospector, our nation's money supply would have shut down. By prospecting for gold, one added to the nation's wealth and showed the world what had made this country so great and allowed it to industrialize as quickly as it had.

Every year streams and rivers had been 're-salted' or replenished with gold that had been brought to the surface of the earth by wind, water, fire and ice and then harvested by many. Floods often replenished most of the gold on our earth, as well as volcanic eruptions.

Nowadays, gold has been melted down in small firebrick furnaces containing a graphite crucible. Pouring the gold out of the crucible with long steel tongs into a cone-shaped mold called a 'steel button' allowed the gold to cool into a 'button of gold'. This made it easier for the refiner to keep from losing the gold in fine granular amounts.

Nuggets were rarely melted down; considered small works of art; they had their own unique, sculptured signatures. No two nuggets were ever alike and an assayer could usually tell what river they came from due to their unique shapes.

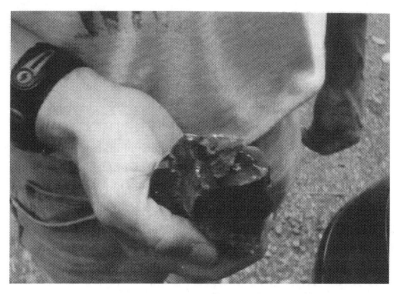

John Davis with a White River Mine sample
loaded with Fools Gold © 2004

Section 5
Aqua regia ("The Royal Water")

Aqua regia or "Royal Water" received its name centuries ago due to its ability to have dissolved the 'metal of kings', gold, silver and platinum into solution.

Chemists discovered that mixing nitric acid with hydrochloric acid produced an acid so strong it could burn through thick steel plates and keep on going until it was diluted by water. Up until the current day no other acid could successfully melt precious metals from rocks or from other metals. Therefore, the use of *Aqua regia* was both successful for mining and for recycling.

WARNING: The use of acids has been VERY DANGEROUS, used in laboratories under safe conditions, along with the supervision of licensed, expert chemists. Since 1994 the author of this book HAD NOT CONDONED the use of such methods for leaching precious metals for mining or for recycling purposes. This information had been offered for INFORMATIONAL PURPOSES ONLY. He recommended that readers not try this at home or at work, or under any unsafe condition without expert help and guidance.

Websites devoted to this subject have appeared as public information being shared on the Internet:

http://home.att.net/~numericana/answer/chemistry.htm

http://www.bartleby.com/65/aq/aquaregi.html

Extracting Gold from Scrap Computers and Old Cell Phones and Pagers Aqua Regia Dissolves Gold

Since the 1800s prospectors used a method of extracting gold from crushed ore using cyanide. The discovery of another way to leach gold from crushed ore was discovered using extremely strong acids mixed together in a glass beaker or jar. The chemical reaction created extreme heat and toxic fumes. It was a mix of one- part nitric acid with one-part hydrochloric acid to make *Aqua regia* (Royal Water) plus gold. This created nitrogen dioxide and chloroauric acid...from which chemists extracted pure gold (gold salt) as a precipitate. Once the reaction had stopped bubbling, the solution resembled a bile-colored (yellow-green) mixture. It was chloroauric acid. Having added some scrap magnesium to the solution made it slowly react (for several hours) and bubble and turn a mustard-color...with the gold precipitating out as a salt. Chemists would then rinse the solution thoroughly with distilled water....and the gold dropped to the bottom (precipitated out). The liquid was then poured out in order to allow the gold powder (yellow-to-dark brown colored) to dry and be stored safely in a tight, dry container.

Section 6
Of Life, Liberty, and the Protection of Fish Eggs

The debate between environmentalists and miners heated up in the early 1970s in the United States and continued to modern day. Those in the "Green Movement" began labeling those outside of the movement as "not-caring" for the environment. Reflecting on the miners' use of water monitors in the late 1800s (from both photos and movies), which washed down whole mountains and trees, the "Greenies" had valid ammunition to stake their claims. "They" claimed that "miners" were destroying the landscape and its animals and fish by using equipment and methods that were outdated and harmful to the environment.

"They" pointed out, validly, that the use of poisonous mercury by early miners for amalgamating gold concentrates for later smelting caused severe environmental damage. Much of that mercury had washed out of gold pans and had sunk into the sands and gravels of major streams and rivers. (Much of this evidence remained undiscovered until today and continued to be cleaned up by dredgers. At $70.00 per one-pound flask it paid to find it and clean it up!) Mercury was poisonous to humans when it touched skin or its fumes were inhaled.

Because of this common knowledge the "Greenies" transferred this poisoning capability onto fish. They were correct. It became illegal to use mercury in mining near streams and rivers. This situation has remained to this day.

The protection of salmon as an endangered species had become another nail in the recreational mining coffin, as miners struggled with the effects of previous mining methodologies. The main mantra that had been successfully used by environmentalists and government officials had been that salmon eggs 'be protected at all costs from land developers, miners, farmers and loggers.' Years of study by the government and private foundations and universities resulted in a "fix" for the salmon problem.

Beginning in the early 1980s the fix was put into full force. Efforts were made to close logging roads 'due to silt washing downhill from deforestation into streams and rivers, resulting in the covering of salmon eggs'; further efforts were enforced to keep ATV and motorcycle riders out (for the same reason just noted), including small-scale miners. Farmers were discouraged from 'using poisonous fertilizers that might wash downhill into water used by salmon'.

It had been difficult for modern day miners to deny the results of the sins of their predecessors. Therefore, a cooperative effort had to take place between the needs of the "Greenies" and those of miners.

Of Dredging, Cleaning Gravels, and Rotting Fish Eggs

For modern day miners overcoming accusations of ruining spawning habitat began to take years. Sounding the battle cry to make a 'difference' against the enemies of water, 'Greenies' successfully used the argument that siltation of salmon eggs was a by-product of mining in all its forms. It was also an attack on the pursuit of wealth.

The 'Greenies' claimed that miners stirred up mud and silt in rivers. The mud and silt covered salmon eggs as they molted. Thus, salmon eggs died from lack of oxygen and did not hatch. It became one industry against another.

Interestingly enough the 'Greenies' had failed to mention the yearly devastation caused by flooding from heavy rainfall, as well as the positive aspect dredging caused as gravels were cleaned of oxygen-starving mud. Normally, fish laid their eggs in gravels in order to allow oxygenated water to circulate around eggs as the eggs matured. However, many eggs actually rotted due to gravels becoming plugged with silt and other materials. It was claimed that this caused the loss of millions of salmon eggs each year.

Along came the saviors of the eggs, the dredgers. Each season when dredging was allowed on rivers in Washington the spawning gravels were sucked clean of oxygen choking muds and poisonous heavy metals, such as lead and mercury. This provided a needed benefit to streams and rivers. Additionally, when dredgers created holes near the downriver side of boulders a natural bed was created in which salmon rested until regaining their strength prior to heading back up-river.

Those claiming to be 'Environmentalists' had ignored miners in their environmentalism. Miners had become more aware of their own value as environmentalists who remained quiet in the political shadows. Fortunately, miners had to come out of their slumber from prior years. Moreover, they needed to remind the general public that they were becoming as endangered a species as the fish the 'Greenies' had vowed to protect. Miners had been robbed of life, liberty, and the pursuit of happiness in exchange for the protection of fish eggs!

Congress affirmed miners' rights to 'prospect' and 'mine' on public lands 133 years ago when they passed the Mining Act of 1872. In that law, mining was seen as a right, not a privilege. Using words as weapons the 'Greenies' attacked the word "recreational" when used in conjunction with small-scale mining. They hoped to make the serious pursuit of gold mining take on the undervalued / non-serious meaning of a "hobby" activity, instead of the serious personal, scientific, and commercial pursuit of 'mining' or 'exploring' for gold. Therefore, miners, decided to drop the word "recreational" from mining. Miners believed that mining was not only a privilege and peaceful act of discovery, but also a Congressionally-given right under deliberate attack. Words carried power and meaning and literally changed the landscape of America, as we once knew it. It was time to take the country back in both geo and political terms.

Of God, Gold, and Guns and Why They Are Trying to Take Them Away

Beyond restricting use of public lands, this author believed that higher powers beyond his simple control had worked behind the scenes for years to slowly discourage and then bankrupt the average citizen from participating in his / her God-given right to worship God, prospect for and profit from gold, and to own and carry firearms for personal use. Never before had the American people seen such an attack on individual and collective rights to use public lands. Never before had we, as a people, seen the outright attack on the three things that helped build this country in the first place: The right to worship God, search for and mine and own gold, and own guns!

Miners had to turn to the power of Common Sense while mining.

Common sense dictated that miners perform the following tasks in order to maintain and preserve their continuing rights:

- Bring concentrates home to go through in the privacy of one's back yard
- Pan out concentrates in a large washtub when nearby a river
- Fill in holes, pack out personal garbage and that of others
- Not destroy vegetation
- Let the forest ranger know that you would be panning legally
- Follow the rules in the Washington State Gold and Fish pamphlet
- Invite Washington State legislators out to pan for gold!

Common sense also dictated that miners consider the following if questioned by authorities while mining:

- Remain calm and do not argue
- Ask if you are being arrested?
- If not, walk away peacefully once the questioning ends
- If your equipment is confiscated…it is cheap, and replaceable, versus a long and expensive court battle

Section 7
Customer Comments

(Book Reviews)

NEWS ARTICLES: June 28, 2002

He Is Still Hoping For Another Gold Rush by Mary Swift of the South County Journal-Kent, WA (Local Section) at the following Web address:

http://www.kingcountyjournal.com/sited/story/html/97115

An Online Book Review by Rodger Petrik of Everett, WA.

Mon. Sept. 01, 2003

"Great information guide on how to find gold in Washington State. Worked the Snohomish river system and found gold. Have now really got the gold bug. I am waiting for the next book on disk to come out for more information and places to go and explore. Hope he comes out with a book to go rock hounding in Washington State. If you're new or old-hat at gold prospecting, this is the book for you."

Return-Path: <bobnterivert@hotmail.com>

Disposition-Notification-To: "Bob & Teri Vertefeuille"

       <bobnterivert@hotmail.com>

X-Sender: bobnterivert@hotmail.com

X-Originating-IP: [24.22.248.119]

X-OriginalArrivalTime: 18 Mar 2005 03:45:25.0953 (UTC)

FILETIME=[EBA02310:01C52B6C]

X-UNTD-UBE: -1

X-MimeOLE: Produced By Microsoft MimeOLE V6.00.2800.1441

Sean,

I would strongly recommend your DVD to anyone who wants to learn the basics in prospecting. It was very interesting, and for the beginning prospector, a real easy way to learn. It is more than just grabbing a pan and hitting the river, but much less complicated and involved than one would guess.

I believe that anyone watching your demonstration would immediately "catch the fever". I know when I was finished watching the DVD, I wanted to hit the river. Unfortunately, I have to wait.

Perhaps you could answer a question. Does the permit for prospecting cost anything? The "spots" I talked to you about in our earlier correspondence are by no means secret. I would love to take anyone who so desired to those very locations and let them see for themselves how rich the gold deposits are.

I am surprised that nobody else had ever worked the area (except the early miners and later the Chinese). As previously mentioned, I have pulled up as many as twenty flakes in one pan. Even my children, who were overly anxious to get to the bottom of their pans found a few flakes. This would be the Buffalo Eddy area on the Snake River south of Asotin on the Washington-side of the river.

The other places where I found gold were mostly in Idaho; although, I did find color on Peshastin Creek and Swauk Creek up on Blewett Pass near Ellensburg.

I would really be interested in meeting up with you when the season rolls around. I would love to try my luck on this side of the mountains and not have to worry about tangling with poison oak and rattlesnakes.

Hope to hear from you soon. By the way, feel free to quote me any time.

I'll send you the permission to publish form ASAP.

"Stiff Neck" Bob Vertefeuille

John Davis and his 'Motherlode' of iron pyrite
(Fools Gold) White River Mine

Sean-

Hello, my name is Charles and we spoke at the Gold Show in Monroe on the 26th. I am the one who bought your DVD at Baker Street Books. I explained to you that I was having trouble with the replacement copy. When I returned home yesterday I cleaned the DVD to make sure the playing surface was clear, and after that it played just fine.

I enjoyed watching it very much. It was very instructive and I liked the enthusiasm you put into your demonstrations. Thank you for making this DVD and speaking with me at the show. I found both very educational. I hope to meet you on the Green River someday soon.

Charles zebo@eskimo.com

Sean Showing Off A Lucky Pan of Golden Glitter at Horseshoe Bend-1994

Tue, 22 Mar 2005 16:18:05 PST
Hi there, Sean. I hope your week is going well, I just got the second of three shots in my knee. Lots of fun. Here is my narrative.

"I often go out into the wilderness to look for gold in the rivers and streams, or just to go for a hike. Whenever I do I try to be wary of the wildlife that stalks the woods, such as bears or mountain lions.

Mountain lions have been known to hide behind things such as trees.

However, when I'm looking for gold, I am always more concerned about the two legged animals that like to hide behind a badge. I'd much rather run into a mountain lion or even a bear!"

How's that? Let me know what you think.

Talk to you later,

John.

jdavis98022@yahoo.com

Sluicebox Sean Dreaming of Gold in 2005

Old Diversion Tunnel at Horseshoe Bend on the Sultan River - 1994

Walla-Walla Wa
May 20 2011

To Sean T. Taeschner:
From: William F. Walters
817 North Main B-2
Walla-Walla Wa. 99362-1358

I Just Read your Book Finding Gold in Washington State 2005-06. Do you have up Dates of This Book. I Found This Book in The Library. Please send Me a List of What you Do have. or Rock hounding Washington or Oregon.

I have Been Prospecting Since 1952 Arizona 50+ years or Age 16 When state Geologest Auther Flagg showed Me where To Find Gold up The Banks From The Water.

At The Time Auther Flagg Was President of The Phoenix Az. Rock and Mineral Club. My First Gold Nugget Was The size (over)

③ I Like The Gem, Mineral, Geologal
Maps of Counties The Best or Also
The 1.24,000 or 7.5 Topo. Maps That show
The Faults and Fractures of The Mountains
    Quartz and quartzite which is Mostly
Gray was The Last To Form and The
Slower Caused Crystals. That was Pushed
up To The Surface,
    Even satalite, Areal, Maps over The Computer
Can Give some indication of where To
Look For Mineral in The Red, yellow, Black
zones, They May show, Dykes, Volcanos,
    Theres places in Arizona in Santa Marie.
River Near Bagdad Arizona where There
are Several Mines That have Gold Tellurides
in Them and Areas where Gold Nuggets Can
be Found.
    My Theory is The hot Volcanos Caused The
Tellurides To Melt out To Gold.?
    Volcano Pipes Can have Gold & Nuggets
Almose Pure in it.
    The Faults in hills and Mountains are
a Good Place To Look   (over)

of My small Finger Nail or $\frac{1}{4} \times \frac{1}{4}$ " at
Gold Price of $35.00 a ounce.
Needless To Say I Been at it Ever
since.
   I Am 75 years old and still Good shape.
I would Like To Know More information
on small dredges up To 4 in I have
2 small 2.5 with a old 3 horse Briggs
a Straton Motor, 2 whites GMT Gold
detector and a Test Nugget I Found at
7 inchs in Arizona,
   I Found a Deetector has To Pick up
a BB, from 3 To 5 inchs, I have used
Gold Bug I & II, Minelab, several whites
since 1960,
   a Lot of early Deetoetors would Not Pick
up small Nuggets, Any Deetoctor will Pick
up Nuggets size of a Dime or Bigger,
   I have a Auto Graphed Book By Jim Straight
I Got at a Phoenix Gold show when I Bought
My First whites GMT.

④ Several Tourquoise Mines have Been
Found Looking For copper Minerals, Gold,
other Minerals.

If I Find Blue Looking Ground I Start
Look For Opal, Petrified Wood, Fossles. Diamonds
In Arizona a Fault will have More
Vegatation in it and Greener due To
The Water in it.

There is a Red Clay on The PipeLine
Road about 5-7 Mile south of Salome
Ariz. That has Nice Red a White Desert
Rose's in it of Gypson or Solonite in
it. Use a ¼ screen. For Them.

I believe This is The Red Clay The Indians
Used For Pottery as you can Find Pieces
of Broken Pottery in The Area and it Looks
The Same.

Also If you make any New pubacation you
Should mention That 1938-41 That President
Franklin D. Roosevelt ~~Stopped~~ Stoped The Gold
Standard were you could not Buy or Sell Gold
So Many Miners Blasted Shut There Mines.
I Was Told This By a Old Homesteader

(5)

Miner whom I Lotter Worked with in
Bee keeping on The Santa Marie River.
This is a map of The Area. 22 miles
East of Kingman Take 93 south Toward Wickenburg
about 60 miles To 97 Then To 96 if you
go Left you Come To Bagdad Copper Town and
Mine, Large open Pit.

 Then Go Back south about 8 & 9 miles To
The Santa Marie River & Bridge, Santa
Marie Road is on The Right after Crossing
The Bridge. Then go south, when you Come
To Water Tank, a yellow Building on Left
on a white Building Good size Barn &
Repair Shop Like So

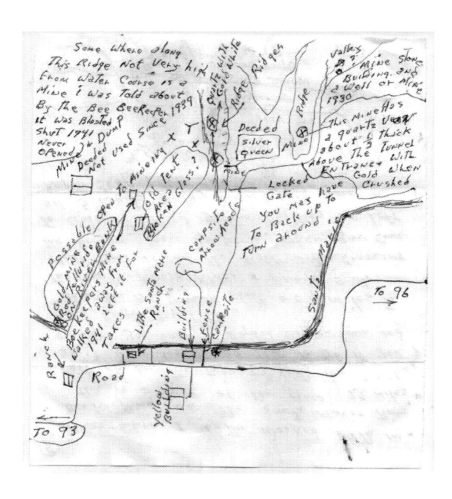

⑦ I Worked at The Silver Queen Mine
who Wrecked The 4x4 Ford and Was Killed
on Black Canyon Highway.

The Mine Blasted shut has 2 or More Green
ore Car Rails on The Dump With Relics
INside and Possable Gold ore.

I AM ONE of Those Poor Prospectors, That
Barley Got By Till The Next Pay so
Never had Money To open Them Most
of The Mines are on B.L.M. except The
deeded No one has Worked The Mines For
Years.

The Silver Queen Property Was Used To Take
The Cats of To Sell in California Till
The owner Was Killed.

I Was deer hunting When I Found The
Mine With The Green Rails Lost Since 1939

The Stone Cabin + Well I Was on a Mountain
and saw it Through My Rifle Scope.
it hard To say What's There.

This is a Area That's Not Visited
Much and Gets Pretty Hot.

The Winter is the Best Time.

if you Know any one That might Like To Go There I Will Show Them The SPoTs indecated Maybe for a finders Fee. ??

William F. Watters

P.S. With the Price of Gold it May be worth finding and mineing. a Lot of the quartz shows a fine Traih of Gold when Crushed.

Dear Mr. Walters,

June 06, 2011
(D-Day)

I thank you for your very thoughtful and informative letter to me regarding your gold prospecting adventures.

I have no plans to venture to Arizona anytime soon, because I am a full-time dad and college teacher of English. I have not had much time to recreational prospect like I used to.

I am considering a new edition to my book in the future. May I include the information you sent me in it? I would need your written permission to do so, and I'd include your name and contact information as the "informed expert."

Many thanks for ~~purchasing~~ reading my book. If you'd go to www.Amazon.com to do a review on it, that would benefit other readers.

I am, sincerely,

Jean T. Laeschner

30844 229 PL SE; Black Diamond, WA. 98010
Traechner@Hotmail.com   (425) 301-3228

Section 8
Clubs One Can Join

BEDROCK PROSPECTORS CLUB

http://www.bedrockprospectors.org

Meetings are held on the third Monday of each month from 7:30-10PM at the Puyallup Masonic Hall: 1005 West Pioneer; Puyallup, WA 98371 Richard Holcomb, President (253) 359-5890. $35 per family. Renewal is the same amount yearly.

BOEING EMPLOYEES EVERETT PROSPECTING SOCIETY, INC.

http://www.beepsinc.com Dues are $25.00 per year. Membership is open to employees and their families only. Meetings are on the fourth Wednesday each month starting at 5PM at the Everett Activity Center, 6400 36th Ave. W. in Building 40-201 in Everett, WA.

CASCADE TREASURE CLUB

http://cascadetreasureclub.com

Meets second Sunday each month at the Highland Park Improvement Club 7109 Hazel Place SE; Auburn, WA 98902. The cost to join is $25.00/ year for individuals; $30.00/year for families. Meetings begin at 5 PM and visitors are welcome.

NORTHWEST MINERAL PROSPECTORS CLUB (NWMPC)

http://nwmpc.com/joomla/index.php

P.O. Box 1973; Vancouver, WA 98668

John Becker, President (503) 734-8557 jon_becker2000@yahoo.com

Meetings are held on the first Thursday of each month at:

VFW Hall 3405 SE 87th; Portland, Oregon 97266

GOLD PROSPECTORS ASSOCIATION OF AMERICA

http://www.goldprospectors.org

P.O. Box 891509; Temecula, CA 92589-1509 - Join for $67.50 on the "Buzzard Special". Tom and Perry Massie, Jake, and Woody own and run the GPAA. These folks have an Alaska trip each year up in Nome, Alaska on the Cripple River. There are also gold mining claims members can work when becoming members of the Lost Dutchman's Mining Association. Lifetime memberships are about $3,500.00. Their phone number is 1-800-233-2207.

They also have the Gold Prospector's Show on The Outdoor Channel on cable television. The current GPAA Washington State Director is Donald Krist.

Donald's contact information: (360) 808-3397 CCSO299@Olypen.com

NORTHWEST UNDERGROUND EXPLORATIONS

"Discovering Washington's Historic Mines" Volumes I & II

by Co-Author, Vic Pisoni, Moderator of Northwest Underground Explorations

(206) 722-4238 4215 50th Ave. S.; Seattle, WA 98118-1425

Tunnelhound@Yahoo.com

February 28, 2005

Hi Sean, Here is our website: https://groups.yahoo.com/neo/groups/NWUNDERGROUND/info

and e-mail: NWUNDERGROUND@yahoo.com.

We have 53 members as of this date. Many of these folks are good references in the fields of interest you and I are seeking. We give reports on our most recent mine related hike and research outings. Dates, time, and location for a pre-trip meeting are posted for some of these treks. Some of the explorations are to surface sites and others are of the underground/tunnel workings kind.

Because of the varied personalities and fields of experience involved, NWUNDERGROUND makes for a consolidated core of information to draw on. I know it has saved me much time and effort on some of my data gathering. Chris has included links to other mine information, and one or two very good mining and hiking photo web pages. From time to time we come up with some really fine old historic photos that are open to our member's use.

See you next time,

Victor "Tunnelhound"

http://finance.groups.yahoo.com/group/NWUNDERGROUND

"This is a loose-knit group of people dedicated to preserving Washington State's mining history through research and exploration and publication. We have been exploring old mines for many years and the towns that once stood nearby. We explore year-round and love what we do. This site was set up to share with people our adventures of exploring old mines and ghost towns all over the State of Washington. So, we hope you enjoy. So, stop in and take a look. (DISCLAIMER) WARNING: Entering abandoned mines is dangerous and could cause harm or death, and should not be attempted by inexperienced people. We do not encourage entering any mine for any reason whatsoever. By joining this site you accept any responsibility for any liability incurred by you or your friends or family or guests from the use of any information contained herein. Also, we do not encourage or condone trespass on private or otherwise restricted properties without express prior and proper permission from the rightful owners of said property. Notice this website is intended for entertainment purposes only."

*REPRINTED by permission of Vic Pisoni for "Finding Gold in Washington State, 2005-6 Edition by "Sluicebox Sean" T. Taeschner, M.Ed.

RESOURCES COALITION

http://www.resourcescoalition.org/

"Hi Sean.

Thanks for your video. I will look at it this weekend and here is the one I put together for our rally in Oroville, WA. I will e-mail you and sure would like information on printing and duplicating services you are using for your DVD.

Also included are membership forms for Resources Coalition, which you can send back to my return P.O. Box address.

My cell phone number is 425-343-5373. We are reasonably close. I live over in Bonney Lake.

Thanks.

Mark Erickson"
P.S. My e-mail is lnlink@Hotmail.com

*NOTE: This information was reprinted by permission

The 57 minute DVD they put out was excellent. I would recommend it to anyone interested in the yearly rallies held by this club of dredgers and small-scale miners. They are actively working to get the lawmakers in Olympia interested in attending their rallies in order to see that the miners are also environmentalists. They are to be commended on their efforts.

WASHINGTON PROSPECTORS MINING ASSOCIATION (WPMA)

http://www.washingtonprospectors.org

2130 E. Parkway Drive

Mount Vernon, WA 98273

(206) 784-6039

Bill Thomas, President

Secretary1@washingtonprospectors.org

First year membership is $65.00 and yearly renewal is $50.00.

WASHINGTON STATE DEPARTMENT OF NATURAL RESOURCES

http://www.dnr.wa.gov/RecreationEducation/Topics/ HarvestingCollecting/Pages/gem_clubs.aspx Current list of gem and mineral clubs in Washington State

(360) 902-1450 geology@dnr.wa.gov

Section 9
Equipment Retailers

Alpha Faceting Supply

1225 Hollis Street

PO Box 2133; Bremerton, WA 98310

(360) 377-9235

http://www.ALPHA-SUPPLY.COM

Bear Creek Prospectors Supply

Chattaroy WA

(509) 995-3179

jeff@bearcreekprospectors.com

http://www.bearcreekprospectors.com

Bowen's Hideout South

1917 E. Sprague Ave.

Spokane, WA 99223

(509) 534-4004

bowens@bowenshideout.com

http://www.bowenshideout.com

Fossickers.com

http://www.goldpanprospectors.com/

Seattle, WA Area

Contact: Dennis Katz

dkatz@fossickers.com

(206) 228-5349

Gold Miners' Headquarters

http://www.goldminershq.com/stores/prosp1.htm

This website lists gold mining equipment suppliers

Renton Coin Shop (They buy and sell gold and mining equipment!)

http://www.RentonCoins.com

425-226-3890

Open 10AM-4PM except Sunday & Wednesday

*They specialize in selling White's Metal Detectors and purchasing and selling gold and silver bullion

Northwest Detector Sales

http://www.nwtdetectors.com

(503)936-1443

7905 SW Elmwood St; Tigard, OR 97223

Prospectors Plus

121 Croft Avenue

Gold Bar, WA 98251

(425) 750-9290

sales@prospectorsplus.com

The Rocker Box

http://www.therockerbox.com/contact_us.htm

PO BOX 1146

Roy, WA 98580

prewco@earthlink.net or nugget_hunter@therockerbox.com

The Following Outfits Purchase Gold

Northwest Territorial Mint

http://www.nwtmint.com

2505 S. 320th St.; Federal Way, WA 98003

(253) 528-1800

*Ask for Jim Rogers. All gold sold must be at least 1 Troy ounce.

Renton Coin Shop (They buy and sell gold and mining equipment!)

http://www.RentonCoins.com

425-226-3890

Open 10AM-4PM except Sunday & Wednesday

*Ask for Dave, Scott, or Steve Campeau, owner

I like this shop the best. Not only do they buy scrap silver and gold and jewelry, they will appraise it and make gold and silver bullion available for sale! Their prices are reasonable!

Finding Gold with Sluicebox Sean on DVD

*All prices include retail price of $19.95 per copy plus tax

http://www.amazon.com/s/ref=nb_sb_ss_i_0_19/177-7262132-5745200?url=search-alias%3Daps&field-keywords=finding+gold+with+sluicebox+sean&sprefix=finding+gold+with+s%2Caps%2C232

Questions: Trashner@Hotmail.com or (425) 247-8827

THE ELUSIVE

"POCKET GOLD"

OF SOUTH WESTERN OREGON

A TECHNICAL GUIDE:
*SEARCHING TECHNIQUES, HISTORY,
UNDERSTANDING SMALL MINE WORKINGS & GEOLOGY,
HARDROCK PAN TESTING,
METAL DETECTING ADVICE FOR HARDROCK GOLD,
WHERE TO GO*

BY
TOM (T.H.) BOHMKER

THE
ELUSIVE "POCKET GOLD"
OF
SOUTH WESTERN OREGON

AN ADVANCED TECHNICAL GUIDE BOOK:

-SEARCHING TECHNIQUES
-UNDERSTANDING SMALL MINES
WORKINGS & GEOLOGY
-HARD ROCK PAN TESTING
-METAL DETECTING FOR POCKET GOLD
-HISTORY OF POCKET MINING
-HOW TO INTERPRET RESEARCH MATERIALS
-WHERE TO GO

BY: TOM (T. H.) BOHMKER

perhap
permission to reproduce
patterns for review
sales promotion

PUBLISHED BY:

CASCADE MOUNTAINS GOLD
P.O. BOX 33
INDEPENDENCE, OR 97351

PHONE (503) 606-9895

Section 10
Washington State Department of Land and Minerals

http://www.dnr.wa.gov/RecreationEducation/Topics/ HarvestingCollecting/Pages/mineral_collecting.aspx

This is the website to contact for information on how to buy photos and maps, acquire mining claim forms, and find regulations in regards to mining and staking a claim.

P.O. Box 47014; Olympia, WA 98504-7014

Phone (360) 902-1600

*NOTE: Reprinted by permission of Washington State Department of Fish & Wildlife and the Washington State Department of Natural Resources Geology Library

Section 11
Washington State
Department of Fisheries

http://wdfw.wa.gov/habitat/goldfish/ or http://wdfw.wa.gov/licensing/mining/

This website deals with gold panning, how to obtain a Gold and Fish permit. The printable brochure covers the rules for prospecting and placer mining for minerals and gems.

(360) 902-2464 licensing@dfw.wa.gov

Snail Mail:

WDFW - Licensing Division

600 Capitol Way N.; Olympia, WA 98501-1091

*NOTE: Reprinted by permission of Washington State Department of Fish & Wildlife and the Washington State Department of Natural Resources Geology Library

Section 12
Where to Find Gold
in Washington State
(Author's Favorite Holes)

Bear Gap Mine

I was lucky enough to travel with John Davis and his wife and son to explore an old mine about one hour's drive time and a quarter-mile distance from Bear Gap on Highway 410 East out of Enumclaw, Washington.

Arriving at a hairpin turn by a guardrail some 40 feet west of the Bear Gap sign (it is blue and white)…we drove over a very bumpy dirt road until we came to a clearing right in front of a hole under a large tree. This was the mine entrance. We discovered remnants of an old rusted mine car slightly buried under the cave's narrow-slit eye-shaped entrance.

A shard of old railroad rail was visible poking up out of the ground by a large tailings pile some twenty-five feet from the mine's entrance.

Hunters drove by as they searched to set up camp during while elk hunting.

The rock on the outside was very hard quartz-iron ore mixture with streaks of small iron pyrite veins running through and dotting the inside of the rocks.

Venturing inside it was clear that there were no bats, rats, bear, or cougars. Some bear bottles littered the mine's floor, as well as rotting log timbers that were once used within the mine. Old wooden slats graced the floor where rails were once fastened. Small drips of water emanated from the ceiling and calcium carbonate and copper sulfate leached from the rocks to form a greenish Comet cleanser-appearing powder. Moths dotted the inside walls...some alive and others dead with mold shards growing off of them like pine needles stabbing out of voodoo dolls.

Using an LED headlamp and hand-held flashlight, John and I ventured some forty-feet into the mine. The floor was somewhat wet and level and tunnels branched off into five directions. Using a pick we tried to free some fine pyrite samples and made sparks that would set fear into any gas station attendant filling propane bottles. We did not pass out from any invisible, odorless poisoned gas (Black Damp), did not need any canaries, and did not fear any parts of the ceiling caving in. It was, however, cold inside.

It has never been recommended that anyone go into an abandoned mine without a hardhat, good flashlight(s), and a buddy in case of emergency. A gun has always come in handy in case one ran into a bear or cougar.

We did come home, though, with some interesting samples of very bright and flashy silver-streaked rocks. My intention was to have geologists verify their contents.

I had the samples assayed that we found by Jerry's Rock & Gem shop in Renton, Washington. The majority of the samples showed Galena (lead), white quartz, iron, copper, and iron pyrite. No gold or silver were anywhere in the samples.

The owner of Jerry's Rock & Gem, Glen, stated that he had spoken to an old timer from the area that had once mined in the area. The Bear Gap mine had been a lead mine in its heyday.

DISCLAIMER: The author has never condoned or suggested that ANYONE enter an abandoned mine. Abandoned mines have always been extremely dangerous. To do such has always been at one's own personal risk. The author has never taken responsibility whatsoever for the actions of those having read his book nor having decided to try it against his advice.

STAY SAFE BY STAYING OUT!

Entrance to the Bear Gap Mine, 2004

Gold Bar, WA has always been located on Highway 2 East of Everett, WA. As one drove north on Interstate-5, he or she would take Highway 2 east-bound to the town of Gold Bar. A half-mile out of town there has stood a very long two-lane bridge crossing the Skykomish River. About 150 feet beyond the bridge was built a public boat launch where the river-rafters put in and the hard-pack and sand were found to be full of gold! Miners were not disappointed!

On average, one expected to get fifteen grains of gold per shovel-full of sand.

The GPS coordinates: N 47-51'21", W 121-41'30"

Gold Creek between I-90 and Hwy 2 at Blewitt Pass...any stream coming down from that area was full of gold...yet, heavily claimed. It was posted that trespassers would get shot by becoming claim-jumpers. It has been advised to avoid panning here without written permission from the claim owner(s). Prospective miners have contacted the State of Washington in order to get information on who owned the claim(s) and how one could contact the owner(s).

The GPS coordinates: N 47-59'47", W 120-12'45"

Green River Kanasket-Palmer State Park near Enumclaw ...has been full of gold under its rocks as well as fishing hooks and lead. Sometimes, live rounds have shown up in gold recovery equipment. Maybe a gun range was located nearby?

The GPS coordinates: N 47° 18.726, W 121° 53.923

Address: 3201 Kanaskat-Cumberland Rd; Ravensdale, WA

http://maps.google.com/maps?hl=en&q=Fullsize+Kanaskat-Palmer+State+Park+Map.+47.3192904674858+-121.90388917923+16+satellite&gs_upl=25395I25395I0I26719I1I1I0I0I0I0I0I0II0I0&bav=on.2,or.r_gc.r_pw.,cf.osb&biw=1366&bih=643&wrapid=tlif13247 6725609410&um=1&ie=UTF-8&ei=NFj2To-AHYmuiQK5kc27Dg&sa=X&oi=mode_link&ct=mode&cd=3&ved=0CCYQ_AUoAg

Horseshoe Bend on the Sultan River in the Sultan Basin Watershed... on Highway 2 East of Everett as you head east to Stevens Pass was THE BEST PLACE TO FIND GOLD. The old timers pulled 80,000 ounces out of there in 1900. They had cut a channel through the bend to divert the river for a year, so as to get all the gold...but they did not get it all! Bedrock was twenty-four inches down from the river's inside edge and not only were there lots of gold nuggets, but mercury as well from the old timers' gold pans! **Since 1994 signs posted have prohibited prospecting in this area. Obey them. They were most likely private property areas or state/federal land(s) or others' claims. This site was closed by the State of Washington since 2000, because it is a watershed. The average fine for illegal entry**

has been $5,000.00. Not trespassing has been about maintaining respect and a must in assuring the continuation of this centuries-old activity. It has been suggested that all prospecting holes were filled in and garbage removed. This became another reason to try to shut down small scale gold mining in Washington State! One had to develop a sense of responsibility. Moreover, there were black bears seen in the area! They did not wear badges or carry guns, but were just as dangerous!

The GPS coordinates: N47-55'38", W 121-48'21"

Kelly Watson and son at Horseshoe Bend on Sultan River - 1995

Icicle Creek has always been situated about eight miles southwest of Leavenworth, Washington, a great prospecting place. It was developed as a state campground and was filled with three-carat light-pink to root beer-brown garnets below two feet of ground. There was some gold as well.

The GPS coordinate: N 47-34'48", W120-39'57"

Liberty, WA, a town north of Peshastin, near Leavenworth, Washington was still open for gold mining operations on an industrial scale. The area was as heavily mineralized as Blewett Pass. WARNING: This area became HEAVILY claimed.

The GPS coordinates: Latitude: N 47-20'07", W 120-34'44"

Address: Highway 97 between Ellensburg and Leavenworth, Washington.

Money Creek has always been located just off of Highway 2 at the Money Creek Campground exit, about one-mile from Miller River Road. There has been great gold in both the moss covering the large rocks and boulders, as well as in the plentiful black sands. The deeper that one digs has dug in the black sand, the better the gold has become.

The GPS coordinates: N 47.728996, W-121.4081577

White River Mine Entrance Collapse - 2004

Section 13
Unit & Lesson Plans for Teachers

Gold:
Methods of Discovery & Recovery
(A One-Week Unit Plan for 4th Grade Science)

by "Sluicebox Sean" T. Taeschner

CURRICULUM PRESENTATION

Curriculum Name: Gold: Methods of Discovery & Recovery

Curriculum Grade Level: 4th Grade Science

Curriculum Type: Pro-active (Earth Sciences)

Curriculum Cost: $250.00 to the school district for 25 students (paper, water, bus to museum for field trip, admission tickets)

Curriculum Summary: This unit will last approximately one week (five school days). It will teach 4th graders the importance of gold as a mineral and as a material to be mined for commerce as well as pleasure. Students will be able to relate the contents of this unit to the Washington State 4th Grade Science Benchmark Essential Academic Learning Requirements (EALRs) and the Kent School District Student Learning Objectives (SLOs). Not only will students learn to find and recover gold but will learn its historical impact on mining history and word usage in the United States of America. The unit will answer the WHO/WHAT/ WHERE/WHEN/WHY & HOW to find, refine and profit from recreational and commercial gold prospecting.

The unit will begin with students being curious about what a gold pan is and culminate with a field trip by school bus to the Klondike Gold Rush Museum in Pioneer Square in Seattle.

Statement of Need and Impact: Students need to learn that gold is a discoverable and recoverable metal, which will excite them in the field of mining in earth science studies.

Students will be impacted in their daily lives historically, recreationally and commercially as they discover the many uses of gold.

Planning Process
Gold: Methods of Discovery & Recovery

(A 5-Day Unit Plan for 4th Grade Science)

by "Sluicebox Sean" T. Taeschner

STAGE ONE

1) Enduring Understandings Desired

Students will understand:

    a) Washington State EALRs

       (5th Grade Science- Benchmark (1,1.1.1,1.1.4,1.2,1.3)

    b) Kent School District #415 SLOs (1.0, 2.0, 3.0)

    c) Gold prospecting as a hobby can teach life-long basic mining skills, which can be used to get a job as an adult working in a real gold mine.

    d) Practical earth science lessons in school can help students move from 'Why we have to learn this stuff?' to 'I can use this to feed my family!'

2) The Essential Questions To Guide The Unit And Focus On Teaching And Learning

    a) Why do men get 'gold fever'?

    b) Is America really 'paved with gold'?

    c) Is learning earth science important for helping you make a living doing this?

3) Key Knowledge And Skills Students Will Acquire As A Result Of This Unit?

Students Will Know:

    a) Basic gold identification

b) How to process the concentrates

c) How to explain what the gold cycle is

Students Will Be Able To:

a) Read a river

b) Pan for gold

c) Recover / collect their gold

d) Explain and demonstrate simple gold recovery methods

STAGE TWO
Determining Acceptable Evidence
Performance Tasks

1) Written: Students complete a bubble map of what gold is and write in a reflection journal about what gold prospecting is.

2) Oral: Students explain what the 'gold cycle' is in earth science terms.

3) Performed: Students pan for gold in class.

Quizzes, Tests, and Prompts:

1) Students answer in a 1 page essay 'Is this important to learn and could I get a job doing it someday?'

2) Students break into small discussion groups to answer these questions and seek insight from each other.

Unprompted Evidence:

1) The teacher walks the room to observe which students can readily recognize gold versus black sand versus fool's gold, lead, or garnets as they 'pan for gold' in class.

2) The teacher asks himself/herself 'Are they excited about the discovery process?'

Self-Assessment:

1) The teacher asks himself/herself, "Shall I have ELL learners (with no grasp yet on English) or severely handicapped students (needing suctioning, diaper changing, etc.) draw a picture of gold miners instead? Or, do they understand and shall I allow them to go along with the class and attend the final field trip or have a substitute teacher watch them while we are away?"

2) The teacher asks himself/herself, "What do I need to change about the unit or lessons the next time I teach it? What went well? What did not?"

3) The teacher asks himself/herself, "How do I check for enduring lifelong understanding in the students? Bubble maps at end of unit? Shall I have the students fill out an evaluation sheet on my teaching method(s) or teaching style for the unit? Suggestions for change from them?"

STAGE THREE
Plan Learning Experiences and Instruction

Materials Needed: 10 gold pans, gold bearing soil, black sand, garnets, lead, gold, iron pyrite (fool's gold), water, 3 washtubs, sluice box, rocker box, 4th grade science book, school bus, $250.00 for 26 museum tickets.

Order of Learning Experiences (Unit Schedule)

DAY ONE: Monday- (The Big Prop) with Guessing Jar on table as students come in (Sparks curiosity and discovery in the students. Sign with 'What Is This?' Fill out the card and drop it into the jar. Prize drawing is this Friday.)

- Teacher pans for gold in class as students watch and he/she lectures about the concept of recreational gold prospecting.

- Students write in reflection journal or small Flip Book about what they think gold prospecting is.

DAY TWO: Tuesday-The teacher asks what we learned yesterday? Explain to students what we will learn today.
- The teacher presents commercial prospecting and explains how to identify gold and other items in a gold pan
- (Oral presentation) The students volunteer to explain what the 'gold cycle' is from their earth science books.
- The students break up into groups of four and pan for gold during class.

DAY THREE: Wednesday-The teacher asks students what we learned yesterday and explains what we will learn today.
- Students get to learn about gold prospecting history by watching a video "U.S. Gold Discovery: The Gold Rush"
(No assigned tasks or homework. The teacher will allow this all to absorb into the student's minds)

DAY FOUR: Thursday-The teacher asks students what they saw in the video yesterday and goes over the field trip rules for safety for tomorrow.
- The teacher asks the students, "Can we get a job by learning this stuff?" This stimulates discussion
- Students break up into small groups of four to discuss this question and write a small one-page essay answering it. They then share it with each other.
- The students are asked to come to a front table to identify gold, iron pyrite, black sand, garnets, lead and other quartz rocks on individual pieces of paper, which are folded and placed into a prize jar for Friday (2nd chance at winning-if they have the correct answer).

This is a learning assessment tool for the teacher to assess their understanding of the unit so far and add or change anything before it is over tomorrow.

- The teacher also wanders the room and observes students as they discuss and identify the key question and answers to the written and visual stimulants in today's lesson.

DAY FIVE: Friday- (4 Hour Field Trip)

- The teacher asks students, "What was it that they discussed yesterday about making a living at mining for gold. Is it possible to make a living at mining it?"
- The teacher takes the students on a field trip to the Klondike Gold Rush Museum in Pioneer Square in Seattle.
- After returning from the trip, the teacher holds the prize drawing (A new gold pan is given away) for the students.

Resources

1) Taeschner, Sean T. "Finding Gold In Washington State" © 1999.
2) Klondike Gold Rush Museum – Pioneer Square, Seattle, WA USA.
3) "U.S. Gold Discovery: The Gold Rush" (A 4 part video series by The History Channel) © 2002.
4) "Gold and Fish" – Washington State Department of Fisheries © 1995.
5) Washington State (5th. Grade Benchmark) Earth Science EALRS.
6) Kent School District #415 SLOs (Student Learning Objectives).
7) (Pretend) 4th. Grade Science Textbook (Earth Sciences Section).
8) World Wide Web (Internet) Search Engines:

    a. http://www.Google.com

    b. http://www.webquest.sdsu.edu

WebQuest Examples: Grades 3-5 Social Studies •

Grades 3-5 Social Studies WebQuests = newly listed since 4/1/2002 A Forest Forever Decide the fate of a newly designated National Forest. A...

...And They Came to the Streets That Were Paved With **Gold** Chinese immigration to California during the **Gold** Rush-1882 Art for Sale Look at art and...

...Eureka! **Gold** Rush Journal (Australian) Write a four week journal describing your trip to an Australian **gold** field and your experiences there sometime...

...**Gold** Rush Players! Write a **Gold** Rush play based upon historical research. Grandpa's Mountain Uses historical fiction for understanding issues...

36% Thu, 25 Jul 2002 06:02:13 GMT

http://webquest.sdsu.edu/matrix/3-5-Soc.htm

NOTE: Thanks to the Kent School District #415 and the Office of Superintendent of Public Instruction in Olympia, WA for allowing me to republish and use their EALRS and SLOs

Gold: Methods of Discovery & Recovery

A WebQuest for 4th Grade Science

(Gold: Methods of Discovery & Recovery)

A 5 day unit plan designed by Sean T. Taeschner

Sean T. Taeschner

STeshner@Juno.com

Introduction | Task | Process | Evaluation | Conclusion | Credits | Teacher Info

Introduction

You are a weekend gold prospector trying to identify the location of the glory hole in Palmer-Kanasket State Park. But first, you need to learn a few methods for discovering gold in that glory hole before you can collect and refine it.

Do you think that learning these skills could enable you to make a living at what you really enjoy doing…being outdoors…and encouraging others to enrich America by becoming a gold miner? Let's find out!

The Task

As a gold prospector looking for that elusive glory hole, you will become an active learner in discovering that gold is a discoverable and recoverable metal. Will you be excited about how this field of mining in earth science studies could make you rich someday or help you to learn a real-life skill to feed your family with?

You will be impacted as never before as an active participant and peer coach in your daily life from this day forward, both historically, recreationally and commercially while discovering the many uses of gold! Now, let's see if things pan out as described!

You will work with your fellow students to create a special Double-Bubble gold map using Inspiration Software http://www.kent.k12.wa.us/staff/ksd14526/inspiration/inspiration.htm and by searching about Gold Prospecting on a search engine called www.Google.com to help you in your prospecting journey. You will actively discuss what you have learned and discovered, such as panning for gold and telling others how to find it. Let's dig in!

Product to be designed

Students will complete a bubble map of what gold is and write in a reflection journal about how gold prospecting could enable them to make a living as a gold miner. Students will then discuss what they have learned in small groups with their peers.

Students will look up information for their reflection papers by using websites

(Directions to Students) "You will access at least two websites to look up information on gold prospecting for your reflection papers. Click on the website hyperlinks below that are in blue or purple." **WebQuest Examples: Grades 3-5 Social Studies** and http://www.Google.com

"You will also use the following link in Inspiration Software to create your Double Bubble map.

http://www.kent.k12.wa.us/staff/ksd14526/inspiration/inspiration.htm

The final product will involve using Inspiration, and Microsoft Word.

The Process
Student Performance Tasks

1) Written: Students complete a bubble map of what gold is and write in a reflection journal about what gold prospecting is. Could they use these skills to get a job someday working as a gold miner? They will use a double-bubble map format using Inspiration Software at the following web-link:
   http://www.kent.k12.wa.us/staff/ksd14526/inspiration/inspiration.htm
2) Oral: Students explain what the 'gold cycle' is in earth science terms.
3) Performed: Students pan for gold in class.

Quizzes, Tests, and Prompts

1) Students answer in a 1 page essay 'Is this important to learn and could I get a job doing it someday?'
2) Students break into small discussion groups to answer these questions and seek insight from each other.

Non-Direct Teacher Tasks

1) The teacher walks the room to observe which students can readily recognize gold versus black sand versus fool's gold, lead, or garnets as they 'pan for gold' in class.
2) The teacher asks himself/herself 'Are they excited about the discovery process?'

Plan Learning Experiences And Instruction

Materials Needed: 10 gold pans, gold bearing soil, black sand, garnets, lead, gold, iron pyrite (fool's gold), water, 3 washtubs, sluice box, rocker box, 4th grade science book, school bus, $250.00 for 26 museum tickets.

Order of Learning Experiences (Unit Schedule)

DAY ONE: Monday- (The Big Prop) with Guessing Jar on table as students come in (Sparks curiosity and discovery in the students. Sign with 'What Is This?" Fill out the card and drop it into the jar. Prize drawing is this Friday.)
- Teacher pans for gold in class as students watch and he/she lectures about the concept of recreational gold prospecting.
- Students write in reflection journal or small Flip Book about what they think gold prospecting is.

DAY TWO: Tuesday-The teacher asks what we learned yesterday? Explain to students what we will learn today.
- The teacher presents commercial prospecting and explains how to identify gold and other items in a gold pan
- (Oral presentation) The students volunteer to explain what the 'gold cycle' is from their earth science books.

- The students break up into groups of four and pan for gold during class.

DAY THREE: Wednesday-The teacher asks students what we learned yesterday and explains what we will learn today.
- Students get to learn about gold prospecting history by watching a video "U.S. Gold Discovery: The Gold Rush"
(No assigned tasks or homework. The teacher will allow this all to absorb into the student's minds)

DAY FOUR: Thursday-The teacher asks students what they saw in the video yesterday and goes over the field trip rules for safety for tomorrow.
- The teacher asks the students, "Can we get a job by learning this stuff?" This stimulates discussion
- Students break up into small groups of four to discuss this question and write a small one-page essay answering it. They then share it with each other.
- The students are asked to come to a front table to identify gold, iron pyrite, black sand, garnets, lead and other quartz rocks on individual pieces of paper, which are folded and placed into a prize jar for Friday (2nd chance at winning-if they have the correct answer).

This is a learning assessment tool for the teacher to assess their understanding of the unit so far and add or change anything before it is over tomorrow.

- The teacher also wanders the room and observes students as they discuss and identify the key question and answers to the written and visual stimulants in today's lesson.

DAY FIVE: Friday- (4 Hour Field Trip)

- The teacher asks students, "What was it that they discussed yesterday about making a living at mining for gold. Is it possible to make a living at mining it?"
- The teacher takes the students on a field trip to the Klondike Gold Rush Museum in Pioneer Square in Seattle.
- After returning from the trip, the teacher holds the prize drawing (A new gold pan is given away) for the students.

Evaluation (Grading Rubric)

Performance will be evaluated for a common grade for group work and individual work as follows:

Each white area= 5 points	Beginning 25 pts max	Developing 25 pts max	Accomplished 25 pts max	Exemplary 25 pts max	Score 100%
Written: Students complete a bubble map of what gold is and write in a reflection journal about what gold prospecting is. Could they use these skills to get a job someday working as a gold miner?	Double-Bubble Map is handed in.	Double-Bubble Map is made on a PC.	Double-Bubble Map is made on a PC in full color, done accurately, and is descriptive. The reflection journal is turned in.	Double-Bubble Map is made on a PC in full color, done accurately, is descriptive, and compares & contrasts gold to fool's gold, garnets, and lead. Skills to get a job someday working as a gold miner are included in the reflection journal on gold prospecting.	

Oral: Students explain what the 'gold cycle' is in earth science terms.	Student understands that gold can be recycled like water or rocks or air.	Student understands that gold can be recycled like water or rocks or air and can explain it on paper.	Student understands that gold can be recycled like water or rocks or air and can explain it on paper and out loud to classmates.	Student understands that gold can be recycled like water or rocks or air, can explain it orally with peers and in writing and can teach it to the class.	
Performed: Students pan for gold in class.	Student tries to pan for gold.	Students pan for gold and can separate black sand from gold in the pan.	Students pan for gold and can separate black sand from gold in the pan, as well as identify the difference between fool's gold and real gold in the pan.	Students pan for gold and can separate black sand from gold in the pan, as well as identify the difference between fool's gold and real gold in the pan and teach peers about their discovery.	
Students answer in a 1 page essay: 'Is this important to learn and could I get a job doing it someday?'	Student does not hand in the essay.	Student hands in the essay but does not explain what he/she has learned	Student hands in a completed essay that covers the main points learned in class. The paper is hand-written, hastily completed, and lacks detail.	Student hands in a completed essay, which is completed on a word processor, includes graphic organizers, labels, pictures, or charts, and sites resources for information beyond main points learned in class. The paper shows true scholarship.	

Students break into small discussion groups to answer these questions and seek insight from each other.	The student did not participate at all in the group discussion and no reflection paper was handed in.	There was some participation but no interest in learning of the topic. The reflection paper was incomplete.	Learning was demonstrated by active participation in the group discussion and completion of a reflection paper afterwards.	The student demonstrated enthusiasm for the topic discussed in small group discussion and helped peers further understand what was taught for enduring understanding. The reflection paper handed in showed true scholarship and was an example to peers of excellence.	

Conclusion

Key Knowledge And Skills Students Will Acquire As A Result Of This Unit

Students Will Know:

a) Basic gold identification

b) How to process the concentrates

c) How to explain what the gold cycle is

Students Will Be Able To:

a) Read a river

b) Pan for gold

c) Recover / collect their gold

d) Explain and demonstrate simple gold recovery methods

Credits & References

1) Taeschner, Sean T. "Finding Gold In Washington State" © 1999.
   http://www.amazon.com/exec/obidos/tg/
   detail/-/0970843305/qid=1049684321/sr=1-2/
   ref=sr_1_2/002-7688475-1520061?v=glance&s=books

2) Klondike Gold Rush Museum – Pioneer Square, Seattle, WA USA.

3) "U.S. Gold Discovery: The Gold Rush" (A 4 part video series by The
   History Channel) © 2002.

4) "Gold and Fish" – Washington State Department of Fisheries ©
   1995.

5) Washington State (5th. Grade Benchmark) Earth Science EALRS.
   (5th Grade Science- Benchmark (1,1.1.1,1.1.4,1.2,1.3)

6) Kent School District #415 SLOs (Student Learning Objectives).
   (1.0, 2.0, 3.0)

7) (Pretend) 4th. Grade Science Textbook (Earth Sciences Section).

8) World Wide Web (Internet) Search Engines:

   a.   http://www.Google.com
   b.   http://www.webquest.sdsu.edu

1. WebQuest Examples: Grades 3-5 Social Studies •

Grades 3-5 Social Studies WebQuests = newly listed since 4/1/2002 A
Forest Forever Decide the fate of a newly designated National Forest. A...

...And They Came to the Streets That Were Paved With **Gold** Chinese immigration to California during the **Gold** Rush-1882 Art for Sale Look at art and...

...Eureka! **Gold** Rush Journal (Australian) Write a four week journal describing your trip to an Australian **gold** field and your experiences there sometime...

...**Gold** Rush Players! Write a **Gold** Rush play based upon historical research. Grandpa's Mountain Uses historical fiction for understanding issues...

36% Thu, 25 Jul 2002 06:02:13 GMT http://webquest.sdsu.edu/ matrix/3-5-Soc.htm

Curriculum Presentation

Curriculum Name: Gold: Methods of Discovery & Recovery

Curriculum Grade Level: 4th Grade Science

Curriculum Type: Pro-active (Earth Sciences)

Curriculum Cost: $250.00 to the school district for 25 students (paper, water, bus to museum for field trip, admission tickets)

Curriculum Summary: This unit will last approximately one week (five school days). It will teach 4th graders the importance of gold as a mineral and as a material to be mined for commerce as well as pleasure. Students will be able to relate the contents of this unit to the Washington State 4th Grade Science Benchmark Essential Academic Learning

Requirements (EALRs) and the Kent School District Student Learning Objectives (SLOs). Not only will students learn to find and recover gold but will learn its historical impact on mining history and word usage in the United States of America. The unit will answer the WHO/WHAT/WHERE/WHEN/WHY & HOW to find, refine and profit from recreational and commercial gold prospecting.

The unit will begin with students being curious about what a gold pan is and culminate with a field trip by school bus to the Klondike Gold Rush Museum in Pioneer Square in Seattle.

Enduring Understandings Desired

Students will understand:
- d) Washington State EALRs
  (5th Grade Science- Benchmark (1,1.1.1,1.1.4,1.2,1.3)
- e) Kent School District #415 SLOs (1.0, 2.0, 3.0)
- f) Gold prospecting as a hobby can teach life-long basic mining skills, which can be used to get a job as an adult working in a real gold mine.
- g) Practical earth science lessons in school can help students move from 'Why we have to learn this stuff?' to 'I can use this to feed my family!'
2) The Essential Questions To Guide The Unit And Focus On Teaching And Learning
   - a) Why do men get 'gold fever'?
   - b) Is America really 'paved with gold'?

Is learning earth science important for helping you make a living doing this?

Teacher Info

Sean T. Taeschner, M. Ed. is a native of the Pacific Northwest and has lived in Washington State since 1964. His weekends are spent teaching others how to prospect for gold on the Green River near his home in historic Black Diamond of turn-of-the-century coal mining fame. A graduate of Western Washington University in German language, literature and culture, teacher, and a self-employed remodeling contractor, Sean has also authored other books; _Marshmallows With Monica, Finding Gold In Washington State, Finding Gold In Oregon, & Before You Buy A Car...Dirty Dealer Finance Tricks_ as well as a music CD, _Hot Smokey Burnout_ with his twin brother, Mark, who is an electrical engineer doing flight test instrumentation at Boeing Field in Seattle.

Based on a template from The WebQuest Page
NOTE: Thanks to the Kent School District #415 and the Office of Superintendent of Public Instruction in Olympia, WA for allowing me to republish and use their EALRS and SLOs.

Lesson Plan

Sean Gold Panning on Green River in 1994

Sean T.Taeschner

March 09, 2003

4th Grade Science

One – one hour lesson

Preparation

Objective: Students will understand how to use a gold pan by correctly stratifying the material in it to successfully recover gold.

EALR:

> **Essential Academic Learning Requirements—Science**
> **Benchmark 1-Grade 5**
>
> **1.   The student understands and uses scientific concepts and principles.**
>
> To meet this standard, the student will:
>   1.1. Use properties to identify, describe, and categorize substances, materials, and objects, and use characteristics to categorize living things.
>   1.2.
>   **1.1.1 PHYSICAL SCIENCE**
>   Properties of Substances: Use properties to sort natural and manufactured materials and objects, for example, size, weight, shape, color, texture, and hardness.
>   **1.1.4   EARTH/SPACE SCIENCE**
>   Nature and Properties of Earth Materials
>   Observe and examine physical properties of earth materials, such as rocks and soil, water (as liquid, solid, and vapor) and the gases of the atmosphere.
>   Benchmark 2—Grade 8
>   Classify rocks and soils into groups based on their chemical and physical properties; describe the processes by which rocks and soils are formed.
>
>   1.2. Recognize the components, structure, and organization of systems and the interconnections within and among them.
>
>   **1.3 EARTH/SPACE SCIENCE**
>   Processes and Interactions in the Earth System
>   Identify processes that slowly change the surface of the earth *such as erosion and weathering, and those that rapidly change the surface of the earth, such as landslides, volcanic eruptions, and earthquakes.*

Kent SLO:

Utilizing the Scientific Method to Explore Universal Connections
Grade Five

1.0 ...determine the importance of water to the universe using experiments through projects, charts, observations, diagrams, models, discussion, and/or written composition.

2.0 ... to illustrate cause and effect of simple machines, to develop solutions using inquiry through models, charts, diagrams, and/or technology.

3.0 ...demonstrate understanding of the structures of the water cycle, forces and motion, and soil erosion, and soil composition through models, collections, illustrations, and/or diagrams.

Materials:

One 12 inch green plastic gold pan with Chinese riffles
One dishpan full of clear water
Five cups of mineralized riverbank soil with lead nuggets
One classroom desk large enough to seat seven students and one teacher
Paper towels to dry student and teacher hands

Introduction (3 minutes)

Anticipatory Set: The teacher will gain student attention by smiling and pouring several cups of riverbank soil into a gold pan, will pan it to stratify the material in it, then pick out a nugget and yell excitedly, "Holy Jehosifer! Gold! Yeller Gold!" He will then hold it in front of students' faces within inches and ask, "Got the fever yet?" He will then ask students to volunteer to answer the following question: Where does gold come from and how does one recover it and why use a pan to do it? Holding the pan up, he will ask if any students know what the dents (Chinese riffles) in the pan are for?

Communication of Purpose: "Today we will be learning how the dents ended up in gold pans and what they were used for and why they are still used in gold prospecting with gold pans today, and will learn how to stratify the material in our gold pans using water, simple riverbank soil, lead nuggets, a dishpan, and a little patience. Then, after you know how to separate out gold from riverbank soil, you will be ready to go out and prospect for gold in a nearby stream or river."

Body of Lesson
(Learning Strategies)

Presentation/ Instruction: (30 minutes)

- The teacher will orally explain to the students that gold has a specific gravity of 19 on the Periodic Table of the Elements and that it hides easily in soil in rivers.
- The teacher will explain that gold miners have perfected the technique of separating or 'classifying' the gold away from the remaining materials during recovery on a large and small scale over several hundred years.
- The teacher will explain how water is used as the cheapest and easiest form of gold separation and recovery: from commercial dredge, to high-banker sluice-box or to the smallest form of separation, the use of a gold pan.
- Students will follow along with the demonstration by actively listening and writing down questions they might have for later discussion.

- Students will work individually or with a partner at the demonstration table practicing holding and swirling their gold pan and material in the dishpan provided. NOTE: They will have been encouraged by the teacher to help one another stratify the riverbank soils in the gold pan if one student didn't quite master the technique of swirling or dipping the pan in the dishpan's water.
- Once students have mastered the technique of separating the gold nuggets (lead nuggets) out of the gold pan they will take their seats and allow peers to take a turn.
- Students will wait quietly for the question/ answer period at the lesson's end.
- The teacher will work with any special needs students or English language learning students in re-demonstrating gold panning and allow extra practice time if needed.

(10 minutes)

- The teacher will call on students to answer any questions about today's lesson.

(10 minutes)

- The teacher will ask students if today's lesson could help them make money at gold prospecting in their futures? And, is this a hobby or serious business to be considered in today's world economy?
- The teacher will assign a one page student reflection essay based on what they feel they learned in today's lesson for their homework.
- Students will be allowed remaining class time to work on their assignments quietly.
- During remaining quiet time the teacher will clean up the demonstration table with the aid of student volunteers.

Processing (Diverse Learners/ Cultural/ Linguistics

- Students will process the information communicated in this lesson visually as each step of gold and soil stratification is demonstrated, through actively and tactilely practicing riverbank soil stratification independently or with a partner.
- Students with special needs or who are English language learners will remain as observers if they fear participating or the teacher is concerned that they might eat the material samples such as the lead nuggets. Extra time during the lesson or partner assistance will be given to assist such students.
- Throughout the lesson students will be using active participation and cooperative learning to discover how gold is recovered from riverbank soils while using problem solving and critical thinking.
- Students will use critical thinking skills while describing how gold is separated and recovered from riverbank soils in a written one-page reflection essay (describe what you learned today) homework assignment.
- Social growth will be developed through partner work.
- Intellectual growth will develop during the entire lesson with students actively participating as individuals and in cooperative learning partnerships

Monitoring/ Check for Understanding (Classroom Management):

- The teacher will ask students during the introductory demonstration to raise their hands and answer the question of where the gold pan riffles originated from in order to assess if group members are actively listening and interested in the lesson.
- During guided practice, the teacher will wander around the demonstration table to monitor whether the students are able to stratify the soil and gold materials correctly. If not, he will help them

practice holding the pan and swirling it in the dishpan water correctly until nuggets surface and students smile with gold fever.

- The teacher will make himself available during independent and cooperative learning guided practice and student question/ answer times.

Communication:

- The teacher will use <u>verbal communication</u> in starting the lesson to gain student attention using the phrase, "Eyes on me…freeze!"
- The teacher will encourage students to raise their hands if they need to use the restroom, but will ask them at the beginning of the lesson to write their questions down on paper to be answered at a later period during the lesson prior to closure.
- The teacher will wander around the students and use <u>close physical proximity</u> to monitor behavior and learning and encourage those who are not on task to get on task.

Closing (7 minutes)

Closure: (Points to Ponder) 4 minutes

- Who thinks that using water to separate gold from riverbank soils is the best and cheapest way to prospect for gold? Is it environmentally sound?
- What strategy have we learned for separating gold from heavy and lightweight soils in rivers? How does water and gravity work to help us do this?
- Where is gold found in the United States today? Is there any left to mine? Prospect for?
- When is the best time of the year to dredge or pan for gold?

- Why do water and gravity and the weight of gold itself play an important part in its recovery?
- How would you teach a friend to prospect for and find gold?
- Could you make any money at prospecting for gold today in the USA?

Assessment:(2 minutes)

- I will call on students during the closing part of my lesson to volunteer to tell the class what they learned today about gold panning. (See closure above)
- I will assess student learning in today's lesson by having students write a one- page reflection essay on what they learned about soil classification, gravity and water, and the weight of gold all affecting its recovery.
- I will remind them that the assignment is due the following school day and should be single spaced and written in complete sentences.

Follow-Up: (1 minute)

- Students will be encouraged by their teacher to ask a parent or adult friend to go with them to a river to try to prospect for gold using a gold pan, rocker box, or sluice-box.
- Students will be asked by their teacher to consider asking the 2nd grade teacher if they can hold a similar in-class gold panning demonstration for the students in their school. Could they relate it to pirates and buried treasure stories?

Reflection:

- Students will use their newly honed gold panning skills to look for gold, garnets, arrowheads, and industrial diamonds while recreational prospecting or as mining engineers in the future.
- Evidence of learning will be assessed by reading and grading their one-page reflection essays and by looking at the gold they bring into my classroom after weekend prospecting trips.
- If I were to teach this lesson again I would include garnets and fishing tackle as other items, which often can show up in a prospector's gold pan. I would also warn them about the dangers of panning in clay (it sticks to the gold and disappears from the gold pan or sluice box easily) and ask them to fill in their gold prospecting holes, pack their garbage out, and wear life jackets by the rivers they prospect in. Unfortunately, gold prospecting could be an entire week's unit since there are so many aspects of gold mining that have nothing at all to do with the use of water in the recovery process. I could expand on the many ideas of gold separation both commercially and as a hobby and gold recycling, smelting, and mining.

NOTE: Thanks to the Kent School District #415 and the Office of Superintendent of Public Instruction in Olympia, WA for allowing me to republish and use their EALRS and SLOs.

Section 14
Disclaimer

This is an informational book only. No part of this book suggests doing something illegal or dangerous in the hobby of small-scale mining, also known as 'gold prospecting'. The author in no way suggests doing any claim jumping, breaking any local or state laws regarding private or public property (Get written permission from the owner(s) or park ranger(s) before attempting to prospect), using cyanide or mercury or nitric acid to separate gold. It is against the law to melt down your gold. Only the U.S. Mint can do this or licensed jewelers. Entering old abandoned mines is EXTREMELY DANGEROUS and should not be attempted at all by anyone except a professional.

If you bought the CD, or diskette it is for IBM Version computers only and must be viewed and printed using Microsoft Windows and MS Word for Windows. No part or whole may be copied without written permission from the author. Such media is shipped virus-free and use of the media, once the packaging is opened, is at the buyer's own risk. The author is not responsible for any damage caused to a computer(s), or DVD player, by usage in either viewed or printed format.

Section 15
Questions?

E-mail: Trashner@Hotmail.com

Sean T. Taeschner, M.Ed.

30708 229 PL SE

Black Diamond, WA 98010 USA

(425) 247-8827

Section 16
Acknowledgements

The author would like to thank the following organizations and people who contributed to this book:

Betty & Russ Nation of Jade Drive Rock Shop in Shelton, Washington

Bob "Stiff Neck" Vertefeuille of Bremerton, Washington

Bud Neale of Gold Claimer & Feed Conveyors in Oregon

Carl Pederson of North Central Washington Prospectors in Wenatchee, Washington

Charles Burpee of Enumclaw, Washington

Clarence "Doc" Ashcroft of Sluice Box, Inc. in Mt. Vernon, Illinois

Dave Rutan of Oregon Gold Trips in Grants Pass, Oregon

Honcoop Highbankers

John Davis of Enumclaw, Washington

Kent School District #415 in Kent, Washington, USA (for the use of their SLOs-Student Learning Objectives)

Mark Erickson of Resources Coalition

Robert "RC" Cunningham of Northwest Treasure Supply in Bellingham, Washington

Scott M. Harn of ICMJ's Prospecting and Mining Journal (Magazine of the Independent Miner)

Tom Bohmker, Author of "The Elusive Pocket Gold of Southwestern Oregon"

Vic Pisoni, Moderator of Northwest Underground Explorations, Seattle, Washington

WASHINGTON PROSPECTORS MINING ASSOCIATION in Seattle, Washington

Washington State Department of Fish & Wildlife c/o Patrick F. Chapman, Olympia, Washington

Washington State Department of Geology-Library Section c/o Lee Walkling, Olympia, Washington

Washington State Office of the Superintendent of Public Instruction (for the use of their EALRs-Essential Academic Learning Requirements), Olympia, Washington

Simple Gold Recycling

Sean T. Taeschner, M.Ed. © 2012

Get some copper sulfate from any lawn and garden store. It usually comes in a small plastic container and is sold to be placed on plants. The copper increases the plant's ability to grow.

Additionally, find an old 12-volt car battery or battery charger to use in this process.

Get some copper wire (10 or 12 gauge wire) from a hardware store. Get the stuff without insulation on it.

Secure some glass pickle jars or other glass Pyrex dishes from your local thrift store.

Have a wooden paint stick for stirring the solutions.

Obtain a set of blue rubber gloves and eye goggles for hand and eye protection.

WARNING: This process involves sulfuric acid which gives off dangerously explosive hydrogen gas. Do this process OUTSIDE in a well-ventilated area! Wear blue rubber gloves and eye protection goggles. Copper sulfate can burn a person's skin.

THE METALS RECYCLING PROCESS

Step 1: $CuSO_4$ + Electricity → Cu + SO_4

*One must use either a 12-volt, fully-charged car battery as an electrical source, or a 12-volt battery charger with alligator clips. An eight-inch length of copper wire must be on each lead. These work as an anode and cathode to draw the electricity through the solution between the poles as positive and negative ions exchange with the elements in solution. Hydrogen gas bubbles will form and the solution will become lighter blue as the copper turns a blue-green and starts to sink to the bottom of the glass container. Expect that the copper wires will disintegrate as the process takes place. What happens? The copper wire gets melted by the sulfuric acid (H_2SO_4) being formed in the container. Take the nearly-clear sulfuric acid and boil it down to remove as much water from it as possible. This will concentrate the acid to a greater strength.

Step 2: H_2SO_4 + Cu + Au + Fe + Ag → $CuSO_4$ + Fe + Ag + Au + H

Separating Out the Iron

*It is time to drop whatever metals you wish to recycle into the sulfuric acid. Allow the metals to disappear (melt) into the solution. This will leave you with a dark blue-to black solution of dissolved metals. Some of the metals may appear on the bottom of the container. That is most often the gold and silver.

Take a magnet and place it into a clear plastic sandwich bag. Seal the bag closed. Dip the bag and magnet into the Copper Sulfate and iron solution. All of the iron will now form on the outside of the bag near the magnet. Pull the bag out of the solution and hold it over another clear container. Once you pull the magnet out of the bag the iron should be easy to rinse into the container. Repeat this until you no longer see any metals sticking to the bag.

Step 3: $Au + Ag + Cu\ SO_4 \rightarrow Au + CuSO_4 + Ag$

Separating Out the Gold

*Pour off the copper sulfate into a separate glass container. You should now be left with silver and gold at the bottom of your container.

Use sulfuric acid along with electricity to send the silver back into solution. Once it has dissolved you should have a golden-brown or black metal on the bottom of the container. This is pure gold. The silver will be suspended in the solution (silver acetate). Pour the silver acetate solution into a separate container.

Rinse the gold in water and then boil the water off using a frying pan. Pour the dry gold into a container to sell to a mint or jeweler.

Separating Out the Silver

Step 4: $AgSO_4 + Electricity \rightarrow Ag + SO_4$

*You should now be left with a silvery or black sludge at the bottom of the container. Pour off the solution into a bucket of water to neutralize it. Add fresh water to the powdered silver in the container to clean it and stop any chemical processes from continuing. Boil the silver in a frying pan until all water has evaporated off as steam. Pour the dried silver powder into a container and then sell it to the mint.

Printed in the United States
By Bookmasters